Clement Edwin Babb

Talks About Jesus

His Birth, His Life, His Parables, and His Miracles

Clement Edwin Babb

Talks About Jesus
His Birth, His Life, His Parables, and His Miracles

ISBN/EAN: 9783744793070

Printed in Europe, USA, Canada, Australia, Japan

Cover: Foto ©Lupo / pixelio.de

More available books at **www.hansebooks.com**

alks about Jesus.

His Birth, His Life, His Parables, and His Miracles.

By *UNCLE JESSE,*
Author of "*The Sea-Shore,*" "*Talks about War,*" etc.

CINCINNATI:
WESTERN TRACT AND BOOK SOCIETY,
No. 176 Elm Street.

CONTENTS.

	PAGE.
The Shepherds and the Child	5
Other Visitors	8
The Dreams	12
Killing the Children	16
Going Home again	20
Going to Jerusalem	23
Jesus in the Temple	28
The Baptist	31
The Temptation	36
Calling the Disciples	40
How Jesus looked	43
How Jesus lived	48
How Jesus worked Miracles	53
How Jesus prayed	57
How Jesus taught	61
The Good Shepherd	65
The Sower and the Seed	69
The Vine and the Branches	73
The Fig-tree	77
Children in the Market-place	82
The Neglected Supper	86
The Wedding Garment	90
Feeding the Multitude	94
Miracles	97
The Blind Men	100
The Deaf and Dumb Man	103
Peter and John's Miracle	106

TALKS ABOUT JESUS.

CHAPTER I.

THE SHEPHERDS AND THE CHILD.

IT was night, but the sky was clear, and the stars twinkled as if they had a great secret that they wanted to tell to the people on earth. Out in the fields there were some men watching flocks of sheep, that fed on the grass around them. All at once it became as light as day. The men looked up, and there was an angel in the sky above them. He seemed to shine like the sun. They were afraid. But the angel said, "Do not be afraid, for I have come to bring you good news. In the town close by a child has just been born, who shall save you from all your sins, and make you happy. Go and see him. You will find him at the stable of the tavern. His mother has just laid him in the manger, because she has no other place."

And, as soon as he stopped speaking, there came a great many angels. They sang altogether, and most sweetly, this song:

"Glory to God,
Peace on the earth,
Good-will to men."

No man ever sang so beautifully. The men would have loved to listen to those angels all night.

But soon they went back to heaven; and then the men said: "Let us leave our sheep, and go to town, and see this wonderful child that the angels have told us about."

So they went into the town, (its name was Bread Town in their language,) and there they found, in the stable, a man and his wife, and a little child. It was all just as the angels had told them, and they were very glad. And they told what they had seen out in the field to the man and his

THE SHEPHERDS AND THE CHILD. 7

wife, and then went back to their sheep, singing praises to God.

Although the child's parents were poor, they felt sure that God had given them a child that would grow up to be a great and good man, and they were very glad, and loved the child very much.

I want you now to tell me the name of that child, and whose son people thought he was, and whose son he really was, and where he was born, and why he was born there, and how taverns are built in the East, and where the man and his wife had been when they stopped at that tavern, and where they lived, and what was the man's trade; where was Bread Town, and what is the name of it in the Bible, and why was it called so.

CHAPTER II.

OTHER VISITORS.

AFTER the shepherds went away—perhaps the same night, and perhaps several days later—another company of men came to see the infant in the manger. These men came from a great distance. They probably traveled on camels, as almost every body travels that way in the East when they have deserts to cross. These men were very fond of looking at the stars, and they thought that they could tell by the looks and motions of the stars what was going to happen on the earth. This was a foolish notion. But God sometimes uses even men's foolish notions to bring them where they will learn the truth and be made better. These star-gazers had the sky all marked off, and each part they said belonged to one of the nations of the earth.

When any thing very bright or strange appeared in a particular part, they thought something wonderful was going to happen in the nation that this part belonged to. One night they saw a very large star in the part of the sky that belonged to the Jews, and they said to each other, "Something very strange must have happened among the Jews. Perhaps a child has been born who is to be their King. Let us go and see."

So they started, and traveled a great many days, on their camels. At last they reached the Capital of the Jews, and they began to ask every body, "Where is he that is born to be King of the Jews? We have seen his star in the East, where we live, and have come to worship him." And the people all said, "There is no such child here." And the man who was king of the Jews then, said that he did not know any thing about such a child. At last they went up to the temple, and asked the priests there, and they took down a piece of parchment and unrolled it, and said they thought that there was something in it about the child. And they hunted; and at last they found that a Prince was to be born in Bethlehem. So the men from the East thought that they would go to Bethlehem, and ask. It was only six miles off, and soon they were there. It was a little town. They asked the people, and they told them that there was an infant at the stable of the tavern. So the men went there; though they thought it was a strange place for a King to be born in. And when they got to the stable, there was the star right over it, and shining down as if it wanted to say, "This is the place." And when the men saw the star they were very glad, and went in. And when they saw the child in its mother's arms they kneeled down around it, and called it a King. Then they told its mother about the star, and they took out some most beautiful and costly presents, and gave them to the little child.

Do you not think it very strange, children, that those men should have traveled so far, just to see a little child? And that when they found it in a stable they still thought it was a young King, and gave it costly gifts?

Now tell me, what were these men called in the Bible? And what country did they come from? And what was the name of the city, that they first went to? And what book did the priests in the temple read from about Bethlehem? Was it a printed book? What language was it in? Was the little child really a King? And what kind of a King was he? Where is that child now? Can we go to him? Ought we to worship him? And what present does he want us to bring, and give to him? What kind of a star is he called sometimes? And do you know a hymn about that star?

CHAPTER III.

THE DREAMS.

YOU remember the king that the men from the East saw in Jerusalem. He made them believe that he was very glad the child was born, and that he would like to see it. And he told them if they found it, they should bring word back to him. And they said that they would. They could not look into the king's heart, and see what he was thinking about. But there was Somebody, who did look right into his heart, and read it, as well as you read this book; and he saw that the king wanted to kill the little child. He was a wicked, cruel king, and he was afraid that the child, when it grew to be a man, might punish him for his wickedness; so he meant to kill it.

But He who read the king's heart loved

the little child, and said that it should not be killed. Who was he, children? And why did he love the little child?

I have told you how the wise men went to Bethlehem, and found the child, and worshiped it. After they had given it their presents, they went into the tavern, and went to bed. They thought that, in the morning, they would go back to Jerusalem, and tell the king. They went to sleep. In the morning one of them woke up and said, "I had a strange dream last night. I dreamed that an angel came and said to me, 'Don't go to Jerusalem; the king is afraid of the little child, and wants to kill it— don't tell him any thing about it.'" And the others said they had all dreamed the same dream. So they thought that it must be true, and they said, "We will not tell and body about the child, but will go right home as quietly as we can."

So they loaded up their camels, and started away from Bethlehem, and went back to the country where they lived.

Children, how did they all happen to

dream the same dream, and a true one too?

The next night, while the father of the little child was asleep, he thought he heard some one talking to him. And he looked, and there was an angel standing beside his bed. What the angel said, you will find in the thirteenth verse of the second chapter of Matthew.

And after the dream the man woke up, and he arose, though it was in the middle of the night, and he awoke his wife, and told her what he had dreamed, and she got up, too. And they dressed themselves and the child, and packed up their things (they did not have a great many, for they were poor), and started off as still as they could. They got out of town without waking any body, and traveled off south, in the dark.

They had no carriage to ride in, but only a mule to carry their things, I expect; so the man and his wife had to walk, and carry the child in their arms. Poor little babe! to have to go away in the night because a wicked king wanted to kill it!

THE DREAMS.

Now, children, I want you to find out the name of the wicked king. I want you to think about dreams, and whether these people were right in believing them. I want you to find out where they took the little child, and how old it was at this time.

CHAPTER IV.

KILLING THE CHILDREN.

THE king waited a good many days, thinking that the men from the East would come back and tell him about the little child; but, after awhile, he heard that they had gone home, without coming to see him. And he was very angry, and thought that they must have found the child, and were afraid to tell him. And he said to himself, in his wicked heart, "I will kill that child, even if I can't find it. I will send my soldiers, with their sharp swords, down to Bethlehem, and I will tell them to kill every male child there, that is less than two years old. Among them this 'King of the Jews' will be sure to perish."

What do you think, children, of such a plan as that, and of such a king? Would you like to live in a country where such a king ruled, and could do just what he chose to?

Well, the king sent for his soldiers, and told them what he wanted them to do; and the soldiers said, "Yes, king, we will go." It is the business of soldiers to *kill people.* Would you like to be a soldier?

I do n't know how many soldiers there were in the company; but they took a piece of paper from the king, called a decree, and started off to Bethlehem. The decree read something like this:

"I, Herod, the king, command you to go to Bethlehem, and to kill all the children that are boys and less than two years old." And to this paper there was a big seal. When the soldiers got to Bethlehem, some of them stood at the gate and in the streets, to see that nobody ran away. And the rest went into the houses to hunt for children to kill.

Nobody in Bethlehem knew that the soldiers were coming; some of the infants were prattling in their mother's arms, and some were asleep in their cradles. But wherever one of the soldiers found a baby boy he took it, and, in spite of all his mother's screams and tears, he cut its head off with his sharp sword, and threw it down dead, and went out. So they went all over town, and did not spare a single male child that was less than two years old.

Do n't you think that there must have been a great many mothers crying for their children that day in Bethlehem? And that it was a most cruel thing to kill so many little boys, that were just able to creep about, or to walk, or to prattle a few words?

How many children did the soldiers kill in all? Did they kill Jesus among the rest? Where was he at this time? And how long did he stay there? Can you find out any body else whom this king Herod slew? Did *he* slay John the Baptist? What became of this wicked king? How did he die?

What is a country called when a king rules over it? And what is it called when the king can do just as he pleases? Could any body in our country send and kill chil-

KILLING THE CHILDREN.

dren in this way? What kind of a government is ours? Does one man make all the laws for us?

Why have we not a king, like the Jews? Who is our King? Can he take care of every little child, as he took care of the child Jesus?

CHAPTER V.

GOING HOME AGAIN.

THE carpenter Joseph and his wife did not like to live in Egypt. The people were all strangers to them there, and, what was worse yet, they were idolaters. Can you tell me, children, what an IDOLATER is? and about some of the idols that they worshiped in Egypt? What were their names? and what did they look like? Would you want to live where there are no Christian people, and no churches, and no sabbath-schools, and where every body prayed to stones, and snakes, and oxen?

Every evening, when Joseph came in from his work, he and Mary would talk about their home, and wish that they could get back again. One evening, after talking about it a long time, they went to sleep.

and Joseph dreamed that an angel came to him, and said, "Arise, and take the young child and his mother, and go into the land of Israel; for they are dead which sought the young child's life."

Why did not Joseph read about Herod's death in the newspapers? Why did God send an angel to tell him of it?

Joseph was very glad of the dream. He thought it came from God. So he got up in the morning, and took the child and its mother, and started for the Land of Israel. What way did he go—north or south, east or west? And how far did he go? Over what kind of country did he travel?—a country with farms, and houses, and good roads, like ours? Can you think of any body else in the Bible who went down to Egypt from the Land of Israel, and of any persons who came up out of Egypt, and went to Canaan?

When Joseph got back to Bethlehem, he was afraid to stay there, for he heard that one of Herod's sons was king in his place, and he thought that the son might be just as bad as the father. So he went on into another province, that was under another ruler.

Fifty or sixty miles north of Jerusalem, there was a beautiful town built on the side of a hill, with steep mountains all around it. Joseph thought that this would be a safe place to live in; but he soon found that the people there were very wicked. So wicked, indeed, that it was a common saying all over the land, that nothing good could come out of that place. Can you tell me the name of this town, and the name of the province in which it was, and the name of the king or governor of it at that time? And tell me also the name of Herod's son, who reigned in Judea.

How long did Jesus live in this place? and what name did he get by living there?

CHAPTER VI.

GOING TO JERUSALEM.

IT was in April, but it was not cold and stormy, as it is here in April. It was warm and mild, like June. Long, clear, sunny days, so pleasant to travel in. And every body was starting off. Where can they be going? See! they bring out cloth for tents, and food to eat during the journey, and pots, and dishes; and, last of all, they bring out a lamb—a beautiful white lamb about a year old, with its horns just beginning to grow. What are they taking it for? And now they start, a great company of men, women, and children. They go down the south side of the hill, and sing as they go.

Where are these people from Nazareth all going? What feast did the Jews keep in April? And what did they keep it for?

And what day do some people keep yet in April, because of what happened at one of these feasts of the Jews? And why do little boys like to have colored eggs about that time?

Now let us go back and look at these travelers. There, among them, is an old man and his wife and a little boy twelve years of age. I do not know whether he was a pretty boy or not, but I am sure that he was a very good one. *He always did just what his parents told him to.* Do you know of any little boy or girl that is just like him in this?

The boy was delighted with what he saw all along the way; but when, on the third day, he got to the top of a hill, and saw just before them a beautiful city, with a large building in the midst of it, that shone, in the sunbeams, like gold, and all the people began singing again, he was so happy that I think he must have cried for joy. Oh, how he had wanted to see Jerusalem and the temple! Can you tell me why he was so anxious to see them?

They went into the city, and spread their tent right in the street, or perhaps in somebody's yard; and they staid there seven or eight days. Every morning, about nine o'clock, they went to the temple, and again at three o'clock in the afternoon. Why did they go at that hour? On Thursday evening, they killed and ate the lamb which they brought with them. Why did they eat it then? and what kind of bread did they eat with it?

At last the feast was all over, and the first day of the week—what day is that? was it the Sabbath among the Jews?—on the first day of the week, they went up to the temple for the last time, and then started home. There was a great company, just as when they came. Many of them were relations; Joseph and Mary had brothers and sisters and cousins there, and Jesus had uncles and aunts. And they were all very fond of him, I am sure. When they were coming to the feast, he had sometimes traveled awhile with one of them, and sometimes with another. And his parents, knowing that he was a good boy, let him go about in the company wherever he pleased.

They started from the temple, as I said, and went back toward Nazareth. They traveled on all day. Once Joseph said to Mary, "Do you know where Jesus is? I have not seen him since we started."

"No," she answered; "but he is with some of our friends, talking about the feast. He will come to us, when we stop for the night."

At last night came, and, about twenty miles from Jerusalem, they stopped, and pitched their tents. Mary got supper ready, but Jesus did not come. Then they went to the other tents, and asked after him; but he was not to be found and nobody had seen him. Where could he be? They hurried all over the encampment; but could hear nothing of him. He must have been left in Jerusalem. Oh, how sad Joseph and Mary were! It was dark then, so they laid down and tried to sleep. I am afraid that they did not succeed very well. Do you think that your mother could sleep, if you were lost?

Early in the morning, they left the rest of the company, and went back to Jerusalem. What happened there I will tell you in the next chapter.

And now I want you to learn all you can about this feast that they went to keep in Jerusalem. When was it first kept? and why?

Also, learn as much as you can about Jerusalem, and the temple, and what they did there at nine o'clock in the morning, and at three o'clock in the afternoon.

CHAPTER VII.

JESUS IN THE TEMPLE.

WHEN Joseph and Mary got to Jerusalem, they went all over the city, looking and asking for their lost child. But that evening they could not find him. They had to lie down another night in anxiety and grief.

Next morning they thought they would go up to the Temple. Perhaps they expected to find him there, and perhaps they only went there to pray. When people are in trouble they should always pray to God. Can you tell me why? And can you find a verse in the Bible about God's being "a very present help in trouble?" Where is it?

When Joseph and Mary had climbed up the broad steps, they saw a good many old men sitting together, and talking. Those

JESUS IN THE TEMPLE.

old men were called Doctors—that is, teachers, because they spent all their time in studying the Law of Moses, and then taught what they learned to the people. Those doctors were old men. But right among them there was a little boy, and when he talked, they all listened to him. They seemed to wonder at him, because he knew so much about the Bible. That little boy was Jesus. Can you tell why he loved so to talk about the Bible? And what kind of a Bible had they at that time? Was it as large as the Bible we have? Was it in English or in some other language?

When Joseph and Mary saw Jesus, they were very glad, and yet they felt angry too, because he had staid behind and given them so much trouble. His mother said to him, "Son, why hast thou dealt thus with us? behold, thy father and I have sought thee sorrowing."

And he said unto them. "How is it that ye sought me? wist ye not that I must be about my Father's business?"

And they understood not what he meant.

How could it be his Father's business to sit among the doctors "hearing them and asking them questions?" Can you tell, children? Which of his fathers did Jesus mean? What is God's great business in this world? What does he send Bibles to us for, and give us ministers and Sabbath-school teachers? Would you not have liked to be in that Bible-class in the Temple when Jesus was teacher?

Jesus left the Temple and the Doctors, and went down to Nazareth with Joseph and Mary, and was subject to them. They were poor people, and had to work for a living, and Jesus worked with them, and worked for them. We believe that he was a carpenter, too, and helped his father build houses in Nazareth.

Now, children, why did Jesus obey Joseph and Mary? Do you think that he did it to set an example to little boys and girls? Do you know what he says about honoring parents? And do you know of any child that does not obey that commandment, and does not follow the example of Jesus?

CHAPTER VIII.

THE BAPTIST.

JESUS' mother had a cousin who lived at Hebron. This cousin had a son six months older than Jesus. He was a strange boy, and did not love to play as most children do, but would rather go off among the hills, and wander there alone. He was a very pious boy, and could not bear to see any one do wrong.

Every body that saw this boy said that he would make a remarkable man. He would not drink any wine, or eat any rich food. He would not have his hair cut, or wear any but the plainest clothes. He grew up very strong, and very bold, too, so that he was not afraid to tell any body just what he thought.

When he became a man, he went out from his father's house, and lived in the desert.

He found locusts there—little things somewhat like grasshoppers—and in the old trees were swarms of bees that made honey. So he ate the locusts and the wild honey. His clothes were not made of broadcloth, but he had a kind of cloak made of coarse camel's hair, and he buckled this cloak around his waist with a leathern strap, and so he went dressed. He wandered about in the desert until he was thirty years of age. Then he went out to the towns where the people lived, and began to preach. He told them that they were very wicked, and that God wanted them to repent. He said that God had sent him to baptize all who were willing to forsake their sins, and that God would soon send somebody after him who would save them from their sins. And great crowds would get together to hear John preach, and some were angry when he told them about their wickedness, and some were sorry, and said they would try to do better, and then he took them down to a river that ran through Judea, and baptized them. And the people kept coming, and a great crowd would stand on the bank all day, and the man dressed in camel's hair would tell them how wicked they were, and every now and then one would say: "It is true, I know, that I am wicked, but I mean to try to do better;" and he would go up to the preacher, and tell him, and would be baptized. This was called the "Baptism of Repentance."

So he kept on eating locusts and wild honey, and preaching and baptizing for a good many weeks, perhaps for six months. The people often asked him if he was not the Savior that God had promised; but he always said, "No, I am not he, but am sent to go before him, and he will soon come."

One day, the man dressed in camel's hair saw a young man in the crowd, that God told him was the Savior, and he cried out to the people: "There is one standing right among you, I am not worthy even to kneel down before him, and untie his shoes." And every body wondered who he meant. Pretty soon the young man came down to the shore, and said that he wanted to be baptized. But the preacher would not baptize him at first. He said: "Do you come to me? I ought to go to you, for you are a great deal better than I." But the young man said: "No, you must baptize me." And they went to the water together, and when the young man had been baptized, and came back from the water, he stopped, and, looking up to heaven, he prayed, and right above him the sky seemed to open, and a dove came down, and lighted on his head. And then a voice came out of the sky. It sounded very much like thunder, but it said, so that all the people could hear:

"This is my beloved Son, in whom I am well pleased."

Now, I have a good many questions to ask, and some hard ones.

Who was Mary's cousin, that lived in Hebron? and what was her husband's name? And what was his occupation? And what was the name of their son? Do people eat locusts nowadays? Do the men in Palestine dress as we do—or what kind of clothes do they wear?

What is repentance? Does repenting make people any better? Was it foretold in the Old Testament that a prophet should be sent just before the Savior came? Who was the young man that God called his beloved Son? And what was the dove that descended upon him? Can you repeat a hymn about this "Heavenly Dove?"

CHAPTER IX.

THE TEMPTATION.

AFTER Jesus was baptized, and God called him his "beloved Son," he went away into the wilderness—that is, into a wild place, where nobody lives. He wandered about a number of days, without any thing to eat, until he began to feel very hungry. Then some one met him in the wilderness. It was not some BODY, for I expect that it had no body. It was a spirit, and it went along with Jesus, and talked with him. And the spirit saw how hungry Jesus was, and it said to him: "Are you the Son of God?" And Jesus said: "Yes, I am." Then it said again: "Can not the Son of God make any thing that he wants to?" "He can," Jesus answered; for he makes EVERY THING—the stars that shine, and the grain

THE TEMPTATION.

that grows. "Well, then," whispered the spirit, "you are very foolish to suffer so here in the wilderness; take one of these stones and make it a loaf of bread. If you can make thousands of bushels of wheat grow every summer, surely you can make enough for your dinner." And Jesus knew that he could change the hard stones to bread; but, hungry as he was, he would not do it.

Can you tell me why he would not?

Then they went away from the wilderness and traveled to Jerusalem. The spirit was close to Jesus all the time, but nobody could see it. And they went to the temple, and walked out to the wall, where it was very high. And the people saw Jesus walking on the top of the wall, and, perhaps, some of them knew him, and said to one another: "There is the young man that John said was to come after him—look at him!" And while they were looking, the spirit said: "This is a good time to show that you are the Son of God. Just throw yourself from this high wall, right among the stones down there. You can keep from getting hurt, for the angels will hold you up, and when the people see the miracle they will all believe in you." But Jesus said: "No;" and to show why he did not do it, he quoted a verse out of the Old Testament. You will find it in the 6th chapter of Deuteronomy. Can you explain this verse, and what Jesus meant by quoting it?

When the spirit could not get Jesus to throw himself down from the wall of the Temple, he pointed to a high mountain away off, and said: " Come, let us go there." And they went; and when they stood on the top of the mountain they saw a great many towns, and cities, and farms. And the spirit said: "All this world is mine, and I can give it to whoever I choose. I will give it all to you, and make you the greatest king that ever lived, if you will only fall down and worship me. You have come from heaven to get this world back again. It serves me now instead of God. And you want it to serve God, as Adam did in Eden. You are going to suffer and die in order to get it back again. But there is an easier way—just kneel down and pray to me once, and you shall have the whole of it, right away, without any more trouble."

What did Jesus say to this? And what did the spirit do then? And what is the name of this spirit? Does he ever talk to people nowadays? How do spirits talk? Does what they say seem as if we thought it ourselves? What is meant by temptation? And what is the best way to resist temptation? What kind of a weapon is the Bible called? Has this spirit ever spoken to you? Did you do what it told you to?

CHAPTER X.

CALLING THE DISCIPLES.

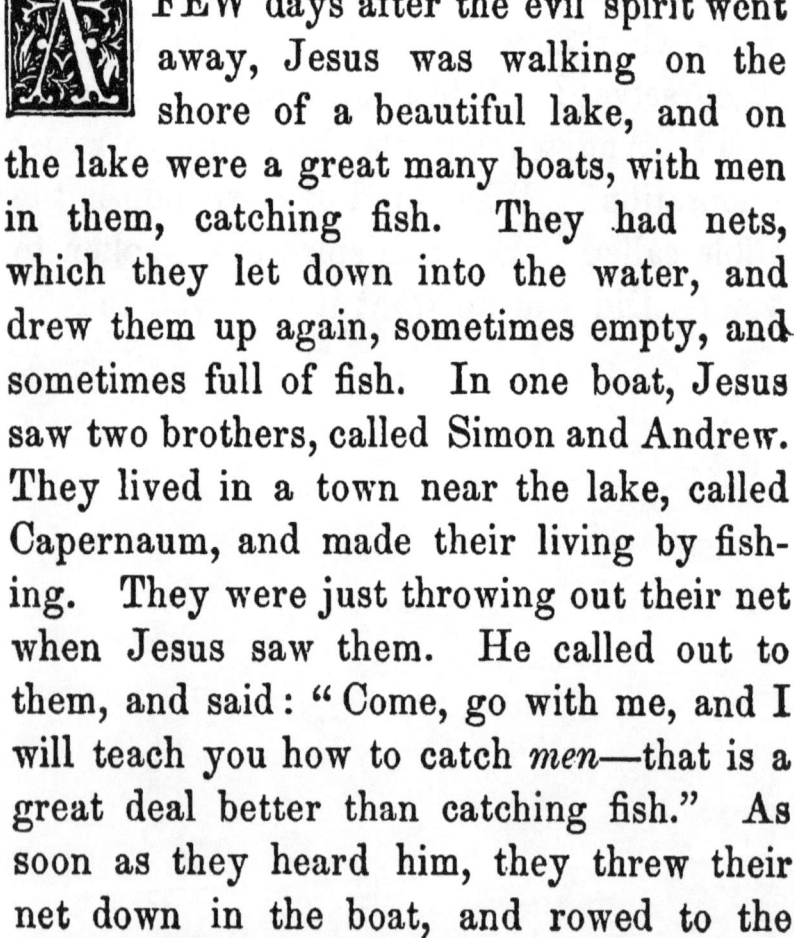A FEW days after the evil spirit went away, Jesus was walking on the shore of a beautiful lake, and on the lake were a great many boats, with men in them, catching fish. They had nets, which they let down into the water, and drew them up again, sometimes empty, and sometimes full of fish. In one boat, Jesus saw two brothers, called Simon and Andrew. They lived in a town near the lake, called Capernaum, and made their living by fishing. They were just throwing out their net when Jesus saw them. He called out to them, and said: "Come, go with me, and I will teach you how to catch *men*—that is a great deal better than catching fish." As soon as they heard him, they threw their net down in the boat, and rowed to the

CALLING THE DISCIPLES.

shore, and there left their net and boat, and went with Jesus. He had no money to give them, no home to take them to; but they followed him, day and night, for more than three years. Often they were hungry, and had no food; often they were tired, and had no place to sleep; often the people abused them for going with Jesus; but still they followed him, They wanted to be "fishers of men." Do you know what Jesus meant by that? Who are fishers of men nowadays? Would not some of my young readers like to be fishers of men?

Jesus went on a little further with Simon and Andrew, and soon they saw a boat by the shore, and three men sitting in it, mending their nets. They were fishermen, too— an old man named Zebedee, and his two sons, named James and John. And Jesus asked them to go with him; and they did not say, "We will finish our fishing, and go to-morrow." They did not ask any questions even, but immediately left their net just as it was, and their father in the boat, and went with Jesus.

They turned away from the lake, and went through a town, and soon they came to a place where people had to pay their taxes; and there, in a little office, sat a man named Matthew, to collect the taxes. When Jesus got near enough, he said to him, just as he did to the fishermen, "Follow me." And right away Matthew left his office, and his tax-books, and his money, and went along.

How strange that these men were willing to go with Jesus as soon as he asked them! Can you tell me why they were willing? And what were they called, because they went with him, and were taught by him? How many were there that went so with Jesus, and what were their names?

And can you tell me something about that lake that the men were fishing in? What names has it in the Bible? How long is it? How wide? Are there any fishermen there now? Are there many boats on the lake now?

CHAPTER XI.

HOW JESUS LOOKED.

WHEN a great man comes among us, we are all anxious to know how he looks. "Is he tall?" "Is he handsome?" we ask. Now, it is natural that children, and older people too, should want to know how the Savior looked. Some persons have painted pictures of him, that is, of him as they think he was. They guess at the color of his hair, and the shape of his face, and so on. Now, this is all very foolish; for if God had wanted us to know, he would have told us just how Jesus looked; and since he has not told us, we must be willing to go without knowing, until we see him in heaven.

I wish all of you would hunt in your Bibles for all the verses that tell any thing about the appearance of the Savior, and, in the meantime I will give you my own ideas about it.

I do not think that Jesus was a *very* handsome man, as some suppose. Some people tell us that the humanity of Christ was perfect, because he was to be a perfect Savior. But I can not understand how a beautiful face, or a tall and straight body, should have any thing to do with his holiness of character. Some of the best people that I have ever seen were very homely. Many cripples, and weak, sickly persons are very pious. They could not be pious if the Holy Spirit did not live in their hearts. And if he—the Holy Spirit—will often choose a poor body, full of pain, rather than a healthy and beautiful one, Christ may have done just the same, and lived here on earth in a body that was very plain-looking.

And Christ dressed very plainly. You will find something about this in your Bible. He did not wear royal robes, like Herod, but wore such clothes as poor people wore at that time. As he went over the country, people saw nothing very grand or showy about him. They did not say: "There goes the handsomest man in Judea!" or "See what a splendid robe he has!" but they called him "the carpenter's son," and "the Galilean."

But although Jesus may not have been a handsome man, or richly dressed, I am sure of one thing—that he was a *good*-looking man.

Can you tell me the difference between being good-looking and handsome? And why Jesus must have been *good*-looking?

I saw a young man the other day. He had fine brown hair, that curled beautifully all over his head. His eyes were large and bright; his face very regular, his cheeks red, and his form graceful. His clothes were fine, and fitted well. Many people would have said: "What a good-looking young man!" But he was going along the street, puffing a cigar, and talking aloud with another young man, and every other word was an oath. And when he came to a muddy place, where a narrow board was laid across, he met a poor, lame boy, with a basket of apples on his arm, and saying, "Get out of the way, you brat!" he pushed the little fellow into the mud, and spilled all his apples. And then, instead of being sorry, he only laughed, and swore another great oath, and went on. And as I saw this, I thought the young man was *ugly-looking*, in spite of his bright eyes and fine features.

And as I was going to help the apple-boy, an old woman hobbled past me, and began picking the apples up for him, and wiping them with a corner of her ragged shawl. And she said: "Don't cry, honey! We will soon fix them all right. There, now, they are clean again! Go sell them, and may God bless you!"

I looked into the old woman's face; it was wrinkled and sunken, but there was so much kindness and cheerfulness shining over it, that I thought she was really handsome.

Now, children, how will you try to be

good-looking? Don't you think that the angels are all beautiful? And what is it that makes them so? And how can the plainest little boy or girl that reads this book look like an angel?

CHAPTER XII.

HOW JESUS LIVED.

UNTIL Jesus began to preach, he lived with his parents at Nazareth. They were not rich, but had to work for their living. Hence, they could not have had a fine house, or costly furniture, or have dressed their children in showy and expensive clothes.

But after Jesus became a man, and God called him *his* " beloved Son," would you not expect him to live like a prince? The sons of Queen Victoria have the most splendid and costly things, even when they are infants, because they are the children of a queen. The people of England give them a great deal of money every year from the time they are born. Now, Jesus' father, his real father, God, is King of all the earth. He is the greatest King that ever

HOW JESUS LIVED.   49

was or will be. He owned all the land of Israel—all its houses and palaces were his. Why, then, did he not take one of them for Christ to live in? or why did he not build one on purpose, more beautiful than any in the world? He could have done it very easily, could he not? And since he did not, he must have had a good reason for not doing it. Can you tell me that reason? Think about it. Study in your Bible, and see what it says about this.

Christ had no home—after he went out from the house of Joseph, the carpenter, in Nazareth, he had no home. He did not own a bed to sleep on at night. Though every little bird had its nest to go to when the sun went down—and the beasts in the fields had holes to crawl into—and there were folds for the sheep, and stables for the cattle, there was often no place but the cold mountains or the damp woods for the Son of God. Think of this, dear children, as you go home from school or from play to your pleasant homes—think of this as you lie down in your nice beds to sleep. O, think that Jesus lived out of doors, and often had to sleep on the ground, with no covering but the blue sky!

The Savior had no money, except what people gave him now and then. He was often without a farthing. Can you find a passage in the Bible to prove this? He was often hungry, when he could get nothing to eat, and suffered just as you would if you had to go all day without any food. Can you find any thing about this in your Bible?

The Savior lived just to do good—that was all he cared about. Do you remember about his stopping one day at Jacob's well? He had had no breakfast that morning, and was so weak and weary that he could not go any further. While his disciples went to get bread, he found a poor, sinful woman, and began to tell her how to be good and happy, and he forgot that he was hungry. And when the bread came, he did not want it. He said it was *his bread* to do the will of God. He went all over the land, healing sick, and lame, and deaf and dumb, and blind people. He did not take pay from any of them. All he received for his kind and mighty deeds was a dinner or a supper now and then. And those that asked him to come to dinner often treated him very rudely—just as if they felt above him. Can you find an instance of this, where a Pharisee, to whose house he was invited, gave him no water to wash, and did not treat him at all as people in the East treat their visitors?

Jesus lived poor and despised—had no home—only a few friends, and they poor like himself. He worked hard—did a great deal of good—suffered much—was badly treated a great many times. Yet he never complained—and all this time he was the Son of God.

Why, children, did he live so? Are people any better or happier because they have plenty of money, and fine houses, and fine clothes? What ought to be the first thing, and the great thing, for people to think about—something to eat, or to wear, or houses, or lands, or money? Will you live, like the Savior, to do good, or like the men and women around you, just to enjoy yourselves?

CHAPTER XIII.

HOW JESUS WORKED MIRACLES.

PERHAPS all of you have wondered at the many and mighty things that Jesus did while he was on earth. He made sick people well, he opened the eyes of the blind and the ears of the deaf. He fed a thousand hungry men with a single loaf. He raised the dead up out of their graves and made them alive again.

I want you to study these miracles, and see what you can learn from them about Jesus; for it is what people do that shows what they are.

First, see how easily Jesus seemed to do these great things! He would just touch a blind man's eyes, or break the loaf of bread, or say to the dead, "Arise!" He did not have to use medicine, as the doctors do, and try and try again. No; a word from him or a touch was enough. Can you give proof of this? And what do you learn from it about Jesus?

Secondly, see how quickly Jesus wrought his miracles. He did not rub his hand upon the eyes of the blind, and say, " Come again to-morrow," and so restore their sight after a while, but did it instantly. Find in your Bible how long was the longest time it took Christ to work a miracle. Then tell me how it was in the case of others to whom God gave power to work miracles. How long was Elijah in bringing the Shunamite's son back to life? How long was Peter in restoring Dorcas? And how long was Christ in raising Lazarus?

Thirdly, see how many different kinds of miracles Christ wrought. He not only healed diseases, but he made bread and wine; he stilled tempests; he walked on water; he made trees wither away; he brought a fish out of the sea with money in its mouth, and so on.

See how many different kinds of diseases Christ healed, and how many other kinds

HOW JESUS WORKED MIRACLES.

of miracles he did. What do you learn from this great variety?

Fourthly, see how ready Jesus was to work miracles for any body in distress who came to him. He was going along the road, very busy talking. A blind man was sitting on a stone by the roadside, and he cried out, "Have mercy upon me!" The people that were listening to Jesus were angry because the blind man interrupted him. But Jesus was not angry. He stopped right away, and opened the blind man's eyes.

Fifthly: Jesus did not work any of his miracles to make money by them, or to get any thing for himself; but they were always done for the good of others. When he was hungry, he did not make bread to feed himself, but when the five thousand men were hungry in the desert, he fed *them* by a miracle.

Most of the people that he healed were poor, and had nothing to pay him but thanks. No doubt there were rich persons in Judea who were sick, and lame, and blind. If Jesus had gone to them, and offered to heal them for money, he might have become very rich. Why did he not do so?

Finally, Jesus never boasted of his miracles. He did not say: "See what wonderful things I can do!" Nor did he make any display or parade of them. He did them when they were needed, did them quietly, and then went on teaching again.

And now, what do you learn, children, from these miracles of Jesus? How many do you think he wrought in all? How many different kinds were there of them? In how many different places did he do them? What did he want to prove by them? Did every one who saw these miracles admit that Jesus was the Son of God? How did the Pharisees say that he worked miracles? Why could it not have been done by the power of Satan? Is Satan able to raise the dead? Or even to open the eyes of the blind? If Satan worked miracles, would he not want to make money by them?

CHAPTER XIV.

HOW JESUS PRAYED.

EVERY body ought to pray. Is there any child who reads this book that never prays?—that goes to bed at night without asking God to take care of it, and without thanking him for the home and the friends that he has given it? I hope not. But saying prayers is not praying. What is real praying—such as God loves to hear?

Christ prayed often—not just so many times a day, but whenever he felt the need of it. Can you count up in your Testament, and tell me how many times it speaks there of the prayers of Christ?

Christ prayed long—he continued and wrestled in prayer. Do you remember about his going away off one evening, and climbing up a mountain, and spending the whole night in prayer? Did he do this more than once?

Although Christ prayed long, he did not use many words. Do you recollect about his prayer in the Garden of Gethsemane? It contained only twenty-one words. Can you repeat them? And yet those twenty-one words he repeated over and over, for about three hours. Do you know the prayer that Christ taught to his disciples? It begins, "Our Father which art in heaven." It is called the Lord's Prayer, and every child should know it by heart. Well, it is a short prayer. It has all been written inside of a ring only as large as half a dime.

Again: Christ prayed very earnestly. In the Garden he fell down on the ground, and his sweat was like great drops of blood. And this was at midnight, and the night was so cold that people needed fire to warm themselves by! Can you tell me where a fire was made that night, and who stood by it to warm himself?

Christ prayed almost always for other people, and not for himself. We don't know that he ever prayed for himself, except in Gethsemane, and even then it was because he was bearing our sins. Do you remember who he prayed for on the cross?

Did Christ pray in heaven before he came to this world? Why did he not? Had he any sins to ask forgiveness for? Did he need any thing from any body else? Or was he not God, equal with the Father? But does not Christ pray in heaven *now?* Who does he pray for?

Dear children, if Christ prayed for us on earth, and prays for us in heaven, should we not pray for ourselves? Should we not pray often, as he did? Should we not pray for just what we want, and nothing else? Should we not pray earnestly for it—pray over and over again—pray all night even, as Christ did? When a little child is hungry, it cries for food. It does not ask for playthings then, but keeps crying and crying, over and over again: "Please give me something to eat." So if one of you wants to have a new heart, you should go and ask God for it. You should ask in earnest—

ask often—ask over and over, and God will hear you. He wants to give you a new heart just as soon as you ask him for it in the right way—just as soon as you show, by your praying for it, that you really want it.

CHAPTER XV.

HOW JESUS TAUGHT.

JESUS did not have a school for people to go to, and yet he was teaching all the time. He came down to this world to teach men, as well as to die for them. The Jews had a great many strange notions about God, and about praying, and being good, and going to heaven. They thought that if they only said so many long prayers every day, and fasted two days in every week, they might lie, and cheat, and do almost every thing bad, and yet God would love them, and make them happy. Can you tell me what the Savior calls these people, that had all their religion on the outside—who pretended to be very good, while their hearts were very wicked? Do you think it does any good to pray unless the heart is in the prayer?

Jesus knew that these ideas of the people were all wrong, and would lead them to hell, and not to heaven. He wanted to teach them better. He wanted them to know that God looks at the heart. Hence, he was all the time explaining this to them, and he did it often by parables. Can you tell me what is meant by a parable? Some things it is easy for us to understand, and some it is hard. And very often the thing that is hard is like something that is easy. When it is, a good teacher will explain the hard thing by the easy thing that is like it; and this is a parable.

When Jesus wanted to tell the people that in order to be good, there must be a beginning in the heart, and that this was but a small beginning often, but that from it would grow good thoughts and good habits, so that the man would be getting better and better all the time; and that would be easy for him, too, because there was love in his heart—it was hard to make the Jews understand this. When any body talked about piety, or being good, they thought

HOW JESUS TAUGHT. 63

only of saying prayers and offering sacrifices. And what did Jesus do then, in order to make it plain to them? He picked up a little seed, and said to them: "See this seed; how small it is! But if you put it in the ground, it will sprout, and grow, and after a while it will become a large tree, and then the leaves will come out all over its branches, and, after a while, blossoms and fruit. They will come easily, naturally, because the tree is *alive.* The sap grows up from the root and starts the buds, and they open into leaves, and so on. If the tree was dead, you might work at it for years, and you could not make a single leaf or apple on it.

In just this same way does love to God act. A man or a little child hears about the Savior—how he suffered and died for sinners, and he begins to think: "O, how good he was! O, how much I ought to do for him! I will try to do something." This feeling is like the seed. The child begins to pray to God, and to study the Bible, and to try to keep the commandments, and to be like Christ. And the more it thinks about him and tries to serve him, the easier this becomes. Love grows in the heart. It comes up, like the sap of the tree, and makes our words and our actions lovely.

You see, then, dear children, what a parable is. I wish you would count in your Bibles how many parables Christ taught. You will find a great many, and some of them very beautiful.

CHAPTER XVI.

THE GOOD SHEPHERD.

I SUPPOSE you have all read the beautiful parable of the sheep and the shepherd. The sheep is a timid animal, and needs somebody to take care of it. It seems, also, to like those that feed it, and to have great confidence in them. In eastern countries there are men who do nothing all their lives but take care of sheep. They go out early in the morning, and the sheep follow them. The shepherd does not lead his sheep with halters, or drive them, but he goes wherever he wants them to go, and they go after him.

It is a beautiful sight to see hundreds of sheep following their shepherd over the hills until they come to the place of pasture! There the shepherd stops, and sits down, and the sheep begin to feed upon the grass.

While they feed, the shepherd watches them, and if he sees a wolf coming, he calls, and at once the sheep all run to him, and gather close together around him. If some careless little lamb wanders away too far from the rest, the shepherd calls it by name (for he has a name for every one in the flock, and they all know their names;) and as soon as the lamb hears his voice, it comes to him like a child. How pretty a flock of sheep must look, feeding on the green hills, with their shepherd in the midst of them!

Do you know what Jesus wants to teach us by this parable? Who is the good Shepherd? And why does he say that he is the good Shepherd? What does he do for his sheep? What does he give for them?

Suppose you saw a lion come out of the woods, close by where a little lamb was feeding, and spring upon the lamb, and begin to tear it to pieces. And suppose that the shepherd should run to the lion, and try to get the lamb away, and that the lion should leave the lamb, and begin to tear the shepherd with his claws, and that the shepherd,

THE GOOD SHEPHERD. 67

in saving the lamb, should be wounded so badly that he died, would you not think that the shepherd loved the lamb very much? Would you not say that he was a good shepherd? Such a Shepherd you have. Do you know his name? Who is the lion that is trying to devour you? And how does Christ save you? Do you not think, too, that Christ watches you all the time? Do you not think he knows when you are doing wrong? Have you never heard him call to you to come back to him? Has not something seemed to say in your heart, "Go and pray to Christ, and try to be good again?" That was Jesus speaking to you. And as the sheep follow their shepherd, so you ought to follow Jesus.

When night comes, the shepherd takes his sheep home with him. He has a place for them that is called a fold. There no wolf or other wild beast can get at them. Do you know that a night is coming to each of you, dear children? That night is called *death*. When it comes, you will want a fold to enter—a place where the roaring lion can not go to devour you. Christ has such a fold. If you are his lambs, he will take you there. That fold is wide, and bright, and beautiful. It is full of trees, and streams, and mansions all along the golden streets. Do you know what it is called? Would you not like to go there when you die? Will you not be one of Christ's lambs?

CHAPTER XVII.

THE SOWER AND THE SEED.

DO you know why there are trees, and flowers, and bushes, and grass all over the ground? Does God make them, and put them there? Or do they not all grow from little seeds? Did you ever see a seed? It does not look as if it would ever grow, does it? An apple-seed does not seem as if it had a tree inside of it. But if you plant the apple-seed in the garden, where the ground is mellow, where the sun can shine and the rain can fall upon it, after a while a little green thing will burst out from it, and grow up to the top of the ground. It is so soft that you could crush it with your foot if you trod upon it. But the germ keeps on growing, and soon it is a little tree, with bark and leaves. And then it begins to have buds and branches;

and after a while it is a great tree, so that men can stand under it and gather from it bushels of ripe fruit. All those baskets and barrels, full of beautiful apples, which you see in autumn, have come from the planting of little seeds in good ground.

If you take that seed and lay it on a rock, it will not grow, but the sun will dry it up until it is all withered and dead. If you put the seed out in the hard, dusty road, where horses and wagons are going all the time, it will not grow. If you put it among weeds, they will cover it so that the sun can not get to it to make it germinate, and it will never become a tree and bear fruit.

You see, then, that the seed must be put in the right place, or it will do no good. And just so it is with what the Bible teaches, and with what ministers preach, and with what uncle Jesse prints in this book. Truth that you are told—truth about your own hearts, about Christ, and about the way to be good, is just like the apple-seed. If you are careless about it; if you

THE SOWER AND THE SEED.   71

do not try to remember it and think of it; if your mind is full only of play, then it will be as useless to you as seed on the rock, or in the road, or among the weeds. It will not make you any wiser, or any better, or any happier. But if you try to understand what you read and hear—if you think about it, it will begin to grow in your heart as the little seed grows in the ground. And the reason is, that you keep your heart mellow by thinking about it, just as a gardener keeps his garden mellow by digging in it.

When you learn about Christ—how he suffered and died for you, and how he loves little children—if you keep it in your mind, you will begin to love Christ; you will want to learn more about him; you will want to pray to him; and you will find a great deal of pleasure in thinking about him, and Christ will smile upon you, as the sun shines on the plants; and the Holy Spirit will come to you as gently as the dew comes to the flowers; and your mind will grow in the knowledge of good things, and your heart will grow in the love of them, and you will be kept from a great many wicked thoughts and unhappy feelings. You will be a good and happy child; you will grow up to be useful in the world, and when you die, God will take you to heaven.

Remember, then, dear children, about these little seeds. Your parents are trying to plant them in your hearts. And your Sabbath-school teacher is trying, and your minister is trying, and uncle Jesse is trying. Receive them into good ground, so that they may do you good.

The parable that this lesson is taken from you will find in your Bible. I will not tell you where, for I want you to hunt it up, and to study it.

CHAPTER XVIII.

THE VINE AND BRANCHES.

DID you ever see a grapevine full of ripe grapes? How beautiful it is, with its clusters of purple fruit among the green leaves; and how sweet those clusters are! But how did the grapevine become so large and full of leaves and grapes? A few years ago, a little root that looked just like a stick, was put into the ground, and the water in the ground went into the root, and the sun shone upon it; and after a while a little branch came out on one side of it, and then another on the other side of the black-looking stick; and then branches grew, and other branches came out through the bark of these two, and so on, until the vine covered a large frame that had been built for it; and then, all over the branches came out leaves, and blossoms, and fruit. Now, the reason that the vine kept growing was, that the root remained in the ground, where it could drink in the moisture, and that all the branches were united with the root. If any of the branches should be cut off from the vine, they would stop growing, and, in a few days, would wither up and be dead; and if a little branch or bud should be brought from any other vine and grafted into this, it would begin, right away, to draw sap from the root, and would bear leaves and grapes, just like the other branches.

You see, then, how it is that vines grow, and why the branches on the vine are so beautiful; you see where they get their leaves and their grapes. If there was no vine, with its root in the ground, the branches would all die. Every moment they have to be drawing up sap from the root. This is what they live on; this is what they make their leaves and fruit out of. Thus the branches would be good for nothing without the vine.

THE VINE AND BRANCHES.

Now, this is one of Christ's parables. He says, in the Bible, "I am the vine, ye are the branches." He is speaking to his disciples who loved him; and every body that loves him is one of his branches; for those that love him try to get near to him, by praying, reading the Bible, and thinking about him. In this way, they get their minds full of truth about Christ, and their hearts full of love to him; and this truth and love are like the sap in the grapevine; they make good and happy thoughts grow within us. They lead us to be kind and gentle, to try to do right, and to make others good and happy. This is what Christ means by telling us that he is the vine, and asking us to be branches. It is a beautiful parable, and one that I hope all my young readers will study.

What is more beautiful than a good child, one that is always pleasant, and always trying to be useful! How her eyes sparkle! What a sweet smile upon her lips! What a bright color in her cheeks! She is like a branch covered with flowers and fruit!

But a child that is willful, and cross, and disobedient, has red swollen eyes, and pouting lips, and scowling face—nobody loves such a child. It is like a stick without any leaves or fruit, and with its bark all shriveled up!

Which will you be, the branch that is in Christ, the child that loves to read and think about him, and pray to him; or will you be the branch that is cut off from him because it does not love him?

You can not be good and happy without Christ. If you try alone, it will be just as foolish as if a branch should try to bear grapes when it was cut off from the vine. You must go to him; read about him, think about him, pray to him, and get his Spirit in your heart, or you will be cast out as a dead branch, that is fit only to be burned.

CHAPTER XIX.

THE FIG-TREE.

YOU have seen figs, packed in small, round boxes. But perhaps you never saw them grow. There are very few fig-trees in this country. Our climate is too cold for them. The few that we have require a great deal of care, and, after all, do not grow to their full size or bear much fruit. In Palestine, or the Holy Land, where Jesus was when on earth, there are a great many fig-trees. They are as common as apple-trees are with us, and the fruit, when ripe and fresh, is delicious. The figs that we buy in stores are good, but are no more like the figs of Palestine than dried apples are like the ripe apples, so mellow and juicy, that we pick from the trees in autumn.

The people of Palestine think a great deal of their fig-trees. They build walls around the orchards where they grow, to keep the cattle from destroying them; they dig about their roots, to keep the ground mellow, and do all they can to make them grow large and bear a great many figs.

One day, while Christ was preaching to the people, he told them a story about a certain fig-tree. A man had planted it, when it was a little scion, in his vineyard. He spaded up the ground, and made it as rich as he could; then, year after year, he cut the weeds away, and dug around the roots, and when the ground became dry, he carried water out into the vineyard and watered his young fig-tree. He expected that, when it grew large enough, it would bear figs for him, and that, in this way, he would be repaid for all his labor and care.

The tree grew. The spring came. It was full of leaves, but not a blossom could be seen. Autumn came, and other people were gathering their figs, but he had none

THE FIG-TREE. 79

to gather. He was almost tempted to cut his tree down and burn it, but he thought that he would wait another year. Spring came again, and there was no blossom; autumn came again, and there was no fruit. He was angry and discouraged, but thought he would try once more. He dug about the tree, he manured it, he watered it. He felt sure that this time he would not be disappointed. But the next season passed, and not a fig grew on his tree. At last he cut it down and threw it into the fire. He did not want to keep a tree in his vineyard that would not bear any fruit. He did not want to take care of and work about a tree that had nothing on it but leaves!

Do you blame this man, children, for cutting down his fig-tree? Was it not right for him to want to get it out of the way, and to get a better one in its place?

But do you know what Christ meant by telling this story? Suppose that God places a little boy or girl in a home that is as safe and pleasant for it as the vineyard was for the fig-tree. Suppose that he gives it parents and Sabbath-school teachers, to tell it how to be good and happy. Suppose that he gives it the Bible and other good books. Do you not think that that little boy or girl ought to love God, and to do what God wants it to, and to obey its parents, and to be kind, cheerful, and useful? Do n't you think that God has a right to expect fruit from his fig-trees that he plants in such good places? And when God sees such children disobedient and cross, must he not feel as the man did about the fig-tree? Must he not think, "I had better cut it down, for it will do no good!"

Last year, was not God very kind to you? Did he not do a great deal for you? And what did you do for him? Were you a barren fig-tree? And is it not strange that he spared you as he did?

People should not expect God to let them live unless they try to be useful. He often spares wicked men a great many years, but it is only because of his great goodness. They do not deserve to be spared.

I want you to find this parable about the fig-tree, and to study it. I want you to think about all that God has done for you, and to begin to try to bear fruit for him. Will you?

CHAPTER XX.

CHILDREN IN THE MARKET-PLACE.

IN all the towns in the East there is an open square that is called the market-place. It is not like our market-houses, to sell meat and vegetables in, but people go there to talk with each other and to hear the news. When the men are not in the market-place, it is a fine place for children to play in, and they often have merry times there.

One day Christ told the Jews a parable about the children in the market-place. He said that some of them were cross and sulky. When the others said, " Come, now, let us blow our trumpets, and play a wedding!" they answered, " No, we don't feel like being merry to-day. We don't want to dance and sing, as they do at wedding!"

" Well, then," the other children say, " we

CHILDREN IN THE MARKET-PLACE. 83

will play any thing that you choose. If you don't feel like singing and dancing, and playing wedding, we will walk slow, and look sorry, and cry, and play a funeral." And they began to form a procession, as if they were going to the graveyard, and to mourn aloud, as people do at funerals in the East. But the cross ones were no better pleased with this play than with the other. They stood still, and would not join in the funeral procession. They were determined not to be satisfied with any thing. When their companions piped, they would not dance, and when they mourned, they would not lament.

Don't you think that these were very unhappy children? Now, Christ says that all wicked people are just like them; yes, *all* wicked people, no matter how young or how old they are. When sin is in the heart, it makes us unhappy. It makes us dissatisfied with what God does. It makes us murmur and fret when we ought to be thankful and glad. If God sends rain, wicked men and wicked children cry out:

"O dear, it always rains just when I want to go out!" They forget that, without rain, there would be no grass, or flowers, or fruit. If God sends sunshine, they are no better pleased. "The sun is so hot, and the roads are so dusty!"

When they are well, they do not thank God for it, and take care of their health, but eat every thing that they like, no matter how unwholesome, and expose themselves to damp air and other things that they know will make them sick. And when they do get sick, instead of thinking that it was their own fault, and asking God to forgive them for being so foolish, they complain, as if he ought to keep them well in spite of themselves.

The only way to be contented and happy is to get *sin* out of the heart—to learn to love God and to trust in Christ—to say, when it rains or shines, when we are in health or sick—in every place and all the time, "He doeth all things well!" This feeling makes the angels happy in heaven. They are never cross and sulky. They never complain of God, but they serve him and praise him all the time.

If any reader of this book wants to be an angel, the way is to begin by loving God; by thanking him for all the good things he gives you; by feeling that he is a great deal kinder and better to you than you deserve. Do this, and you will be contented, you will be happy. You will have a little heaven in your own heart, no matter whether it rains or shines, whether you are rich or poor, sick or well.

CHAPTER XXI.

THE NEGLECTED SUPPER.

ONE day, a man in the East prepared a great supper. He was rich and had plenty of servants, so he set them all at work killing oxen, and sheep, and lambs to roast, making bread, and cakes, and butter, gathering honey and all kinds of fruit. They were busy many days, and the rich man thought that he would give his friends the greatest supper that they had ever seen. He was sure that they would all be very much pleased when they received their invitations, and would come. At last, when the feast was ready, he told his servants to go and invite the people. He sent them to every one of his friends, and they said to each, "Our master has prepared a great feast, and he wants you to come to it."

One of these friends said: "Tell your master that I haven't time to go to his feast; I am very busy; I have just been buying forty acres of land, and I want to go and see it." He did not even thank him for the invitation.

Another said: "Why, I've just been buying five yoke of oxen, and I must go and try how well they can work. Tell your master that I care more for my oxen than I do for him, and that I can't go."

A third one said: "Your master must excuse me, indeed he must, for I have just been getting married, and, of course, I can not leave my wife to attend his supper."

So every body had some excuse for not going, and the servants went back and told their master. He thought it was too bad that, when he had taken so much pains to prepare a supper for his friends, none of them would come. He felt very much grieved because they made so many excuses, and did not even want to come at all. And he said to his servants: "Our supper is ready—it will spoil if we do not find some body to eat it. Go out into the street, and into the lanes and alleys, and hunt up all the poor people—the beggars, the blind, and the lame. No matter how ragged they look, bring them in. I will give to each of them a new dress, and they shall eat my great supper." And the servants did so, and they made the poor, hungry, ragged people come, and the rich man's house was full of them; and they were all dressed in clean, new clothes, which the rich man gave them, and never was there such a feast before!

Now, dear children, this is not a story that uncle Jesse has made up, but is one of Christ's parables. He means to teach you something by it. Do you know what is meant by this great supper? Have you ever heard a hymn that begins:

"Come, sinner, to the royal feast!"

Do you know any body that the Savior has invited to sup with him, and would not—who said by his conduct, I would rather play with my playthings, or read this silly story-book, or think about my clothes, than to love Christ, and have him love me? Do you know any such person? And do you not think that he is a very foolish person? And even if a little boy or girl is doing so, must they not be very foolish, like the men that would not go to the great supper?

CHAPTER XXII.

THE WEDDING GARMENT.

YOU remember, children, the supper that I told you about in the last chapter. Matthew says it was a wedding supper; that the rich man's son had just been married, and that it was for him the feast was prepared. The people in our country buy nice clothes for themselves when they go to a wedding, but in the East, the man who invites them gives every body a new dress to wear at the supper. As soon as the poor people were brought into the rich man's house, they were sent into a room full of clothes, and were told to take off their old rags and dress themselves in fine new garments. They were all very glad to do so. They were as much pleased to get the new clothes as to get the supper.

I said all—but no, I am mistaken; there

was one man in a ragged, dirty coat, who would not take it off and put on a better one. He said that it was good enough, and that the rich man had no business to ask him to take a better one; that he wanted to eat the supper, but he meant to do it in his own clothes. The others thought he was a very foolish man. They urged him to put on one of the wedding garments. They said that the rich man would be angry if he did not; that his beggar's dress was not fit to go to such a grand supper in, and, finally, that he had no business to come to the supper at all, unless he would come just as he was invited to; that if he was not willing to wear a wedding garment, he ought not to come to the wedding. But the man would not listen to them. He was one of those silly people that will always have their own way; so he marched into the banquet hall in his rags, as proud as he was filthy. Soon the rich man came in. He looked all along the table, and saw this ragged fellow among the clean and well-dressed people, and he went to him and said: "How did you come here? Why have you not a wedding garment on, like the rest?"

And in a moment the man saw how foolish he had been, and he hung down his head and could not say a word. And then the rich man called his servants, and told them to put him out of doors, where it was cold and dark. And they did so. And the poor foolish man could only look in through the windows and see the others enjoying the feast. And he cried and gnashed his teeth together, he was so hungry and cold, and so angry with himself for what he had done.

Children, would any of you act like that man? Don't you think that he was very foolish, and deserved to be put out from the feast? Well, children, this is a parable, and it means you. God has prepared a great supper for us in heaven. He asks us all to come and enjoy it. He wants to make us happy there, not for one evening only, but forever. But he tells us to put on the "righteousness of Christ" for our wedding garment. He means by this that we are to love Christ and to trust in him, and to place all our hope of heaven in what he has done for us. He means that we are to be Christians. Are you a Christian? Do you love Christ, and trust him, and try to serve him? And if not, do you expect to go to heaven? Do you expect to sit down at the marriage supper of the Lamb?

God, who made the supper, has a right to say what we shall wear at it. He has a right to say how we shall come there; and if we neglect Christ, and die with the rags of our sins around us, he will not let us into heaven, but he will turn us out into that dark place, where there is weeping and gnashing of teeth.

CHAPTER XXIII.

FEEDING THE MULTITUDE.

SEE that crowd of people! Men, women, and children, at least ten thousand of them. They are not in a city, or near one. No, they are away out in the wilderness—out where there are no houses—out where nobody lives, and where nothing grows but bushes and trees. There they have been three days, and had nothing to eat. How hungry they must have been! Why did they stay there so long with nothing to eat? Why did they not go home, or to some town where they could buy bread? I will tell you why: They were listening to Jesus; they wanted to hear him tell about God and heaven, and they loved so to hear him that they almost forgot that they were hungry. But on the third day they became very faint;

FEEDING THE MULTITUDE.

they were too weak to go home then. Jesus saw it, and felt sorry for them. But what could he do? He had only five loaves and two fishes. That was hardly enough for him and his disciples. He told all the people to sit down on the grass; then he sent for the five loaves and two fishes. The people all wondered what he was going to do. Was he going to cut each loaf into two thousand pieces, and give every one a crumb? He did not explain what he meant, but, with the bread before him, began to pray. After he had asked God, his father, for a blessing, he took up a loaf and broke it, but as soon as he did so, each half became larger than the whole loaf had been before. And then he broke the halves again, and then there were four large loaves instead of one; and so he went on, until there lay all around him, on the grass, thousands of loaves—a great heap of bread. And then the disciples took baskets full of the bread and carried it to the hungry people, and they all ate of it, and of the fishes, too, until they were filled.

And after the ten thousand people were done eating, there was bread enough left to fill seven baskets. A great deal more was left, you see, than the five loaves that Jesus asked a blessing on; so that he made bread enough for all that crowd of people while he was breaking the loaves.

There is something very wonderful in this—do n't you think so, children? Well, they call it a miracle, and the word miracle means "a wonderful thing." We will talk about miracles in the next chapter, and explain to you what we are to learn from them.

CHAPTER XXIV.

MIRACLES.

PROMISED to explain some things about miracles. You remember how Christ made the five loaves of bread feed seven thousand men, besides women and children. I told you that, as he brake the loaves, every piece grew twice as large as it was before, and so on, until there were more than a thousand loaves instead of five. Now, some people say that such a thing is impossible, and that they can not believe it. But they must be very ignorant people, as you will see presently. What is bread made of? Is it not from flour? and is not flour grains of wheat ground up? Then, where does wheat come from? Do men find it all over the ground, like stones? "O, no!" you answer, "it grows." But why does it grow? "Because somebody

sows it." Yes, the farmer takes a few quarts of wheat, and puts them in the ground, and after a while he has many bushels! What makes so much wheat from a few seeds? Does the ground do it? or the sun, or the showers? or do they all agree to do it? You say: "No; for the ground, and the sun, and the showers have no minds to plan such things, and no tongues to talk about them. God makes the wheat. He uses the ground, and the sun, and the rain in doing it, but he could make it without them if he chose. He must have made the first kernel of wheat so, for there was no seed to plant before it was made, and the ground, and the sun, and the rain can not do any thing without seeds.

Well, if God can make thousands and thousands of fields full of wheat every summer, could he not make a hundred bushels of wheat right away? Does it seem to you any harder to make a hundred bushels of grain in a minute, than to make millions and millions of bushels in a few months, as

God does every year? And if God could make one hundred bushels of wheat in a minute, do you not think that he could just as easily make a thousand loaves of bread? Would it not be just as easy for him to make bread as to make wheat?

When people tell you that they can not believe in these miracles (or wonderful things) that are told in the Bible, just ask them if they believe that wheat and corn grow every year. And then ask them who makes it all grow? Then ask them if they do not think it is as wonderful to make grain enough, in four or five months, to feed the eight hundred millions of people in the world, as to make bread enough in a minute to feed seven thousand men? Tell them that miracles just as wonderful are happening every year and every day.

CHAPTER XXV.

THE BLIND MEN.

AS Jesus was going up from Jericho to Jerusalem, he saw two men sitting by the side of the road. They staid there all day, to beg of the people that passed by. Why did they not work, instead of begging? They were blind. It was night, dark night to them all the time. No matter how bright the sun shone, or how beautiful the fields looked, the poor blind men could not see any thing.

Do you not think that it must be very hard to be blind? These men thought so, and when they heard that Jesus was coming along the road, they cried out: "Have mercy on us, O Lord, thou son of David!"

And Jesus stopped as soon as he heard them, and asked them what they wanted of him, and they said that they wanted him to open their eyes. And Jesus went close to the two blind men, and put out his hands, and just touched their eyes, and as soon as he did so their eyes were opened. They saw the light; they saw the earth and the sky; they saw Jesus and all the people around him. How strange that just touching the eyes of the blind men should make them see!

When people have weak eyes or sore eyes, doctors can sometimes cure them; but no doctors in the world ever tried to cure blind people. Only God can do that. And why can God do it? Does he not make all our eyes? And if he makes them for us when we are born, can he not make them afterward if he chooses? So you see that this miracle is done over and over again every time a little baby gets eyes to see with, and that God has had mercy on all of us as well as on the two blind men of Jericho. He might have left us all without eyes, and then we would have had to crawl about and feel our way. We could not have seen any of the beautiful things that the world is full of. O, what a mercy to us, dear children, are these eyes that can look in a moment to the sun and the stars! Do you ever thank God for them?

But, children, though you have each of you two bright eyes, yet you are blind. God says that all sinners are blind, and we are sinners. The eyes of our souls are darkened, and we do not see God and heaven by faith, as we should. We do not remember that God sees us all the time, and that any moment we may die, and have to go and answer before him for all that we have done. We ought to have our minds open all the time to these things, on which our future happiness depends. But we will not, unless God touches our hearts, and makes us think about them and feel them.

Pray, then, to him! Pray as the blind men did: "Have mercy upon me, O Lord, thou son of David, and open the eyes of my understanding! Help me to see thee by faith—to love thee and to serve thee, so that, when I die, I may go and live with thee forever!"

CHAPTER XXVI.

THE DEAF AND DUMB MAN.

WHILE Jesus was walking by the sea of Galilee, the people brought a man to him who was deaf and dumb. The rest all talked to Jesus, and heard what he said; but the poor man that they brought could not say a word or understand one. He could only make noises, like those that animals make. Do n't you think, children, that it must be very hard to be deaf and dumb; not to hear the birds sing; not to hear the kind voices of our friends; not to be able to tell them what we want, or how we feel?

There are many such people. We build asylums for them, and there they learn to talk with each other by signs. The signs they make with their fingers. It is a strange sight to see deaf and dumb people talking with their fingers. And at the asylums they are taught a great many things. But in the time when Christ was on earth, there were no asylums for the deaf and dumb, and the man that was brought to Jesus by the sea of Galilee must have led a very sad and lonely life. O, how often he must have wished that his ears were opened and that his tongue was loosed, so that he could hear and talk like other people!

When his neighbors heard that Jesus was coming along that way, they said to one another: "Let us take him to this great prophet, and see if he can cure his deafness;" and so they went.

And when Jesus saw the man, he pitied him, and he took him away from the crowd, and put one of his fingers on each of his ears and touched his tongue with his own, and looked up to heaven, and said: "Be opened!" And right away the man's ears were opened, and his tongue was loosed, and he heard, and began to talk. The people were astonished. Such a thing had never been seen or heard of before. No man had ever been able to make a deaf man hear and talk. But God, who gave us all our tongues and our ears—who made our tongues to articulate sounds, and our ears to receive them, and tell the one from the other—God could make all the deaf and dumb people hear and speak in a moment if he chose. And when we see Christ curing a deaf and dumb man without any medicine—by just touching his ears—we know that Christ must have been God. I will explain, in another chapter, the difference between the miracles of Christ and those of good men, like the apostles and prophets.

Two things I want you to think about: One is, why Jesus sighed when he said, "Be opened?" Did he have to suffer himself when he relieved others? And the other is, do you know of any one whose soul is deaf—of any one to whom God speaks again and again, and who pays no attention to his voice?

CHAPTER XXVII.

PETER AND JOHN'S MIRACLE.

I PROMISED to show you, children, the difference between miracles wrought by good men and those wrought by Christ. We will look at the first miracle of the disciples after the Savior had gone back to heaven.

About three o'clock one afternoon, Peter and John went to the Temple in Jerusalem. At that hour every day there was a sort of prayer-meeting, and pious people loved to go and join in the worship of God. Now, in Jerusalem there was a poor lame man. He could not work, and lived by begging. This man thought that people who prayed a good deal would be likely to give more to the poor than those who did not pray, so he had himself carried every afternoon to the Temple, and he lay down by one of the doors, and whenever any body was about to go in, he held out his hand to them, and said: "Please give something to a poor lame man!"

When Peter and John came along, he asked them as he did the rest. But they were poor too; they had no money. Peter told him so, and then was going on into the Temple. But he remembered how often Christ had healed such sufferers, and that Christ had said, "Ask, and ye shall receive;" "Lo, I am with you always;" "Greater works than mine shall ye do," etc. He prayed a moment, and felt that God had heard him. Then he turned to the lame man, and said: "In the name of Jesus Christ of Nazareth, rise up and walk!" The man looked at him astonished. Then Peter took hold of his right hand and lifted him up, and the man tried to rise, and as he tried, his feet and ankles became strong, and in a moment he was leaping all about with joy. How pleasant it must have been to him to be able to walk, after lying on his bed for years! No wonder that he praised God.

You see that Peter did not use any medicine. He just lifted the man up, and he was well right away. The miracle was done just as quickly as those that Christ himself did, and just as easily. What, then, was the difference? What did Christ say when he healed people, or made the dead alive? Did he say: "In the name of God, I bid you rise, or be well?" No; but he said: "Be opened!" "Be healed!" "*I* say unto thee, arise!" He spake just as if he himself had power to cure diseases and to raise the dead. But when Peter wanted to heal the lame man, he said: "In the name of Jesus Christ of Nazareth!" He knew that he could not do any thing of himself, but believed that Christ could hear him, and could heal the man, just as he used to heal people when on earth. And in the name of Christ the man *was* healed. Christ did it, and not Peter.

So you see that the miracles which the disciples did showed Christ's power and his goodness just as much as those that he did himself. Peter told the people so in the

Temple that very afternoon. Get your Bibles, and read what he said, in the third chapter of Acts.

If Christ had not been God, it would have been wicked for him to pretend to heal people in his own name. If he had been a man only, or even an angel, he would have had to pray, as Peter did, and to have said: "I heal you in the name of God." "God does it because I pray to him." But Christ always said that he had power in himself to do these miracles, and he *did them;* and that is one of the ways in which we know that he was really the Son of God. If he had not been God, he could not have done such things in his own name, and God would not have done it for him, while he was telling a lie—while he was pretending to be Divine when he was not.

www.ingramcontent.com/pod-product-compliance
Lightning Source LLC
Chambersburg PA
CBHW031405160426
43196CB00007B/905